This journal belongs to

Betsy Sellers

DELIGHT
YOURSELF
IN THE
LORD AND
HE WILL
GIVE
YOU THE
DESIRES
OF YOUR
HEART.

PSALM
37:4
NASB

You Are
Beautiful
In
His Sight

BELLE
CITY
GIFTS

Belle City Gifts

Racine, Wisconsin, USA

Belle City Gifts is an imprint of BroadStreet Publishing Group LLC.

Broadstreetpublishing.com

You Are Beautiful *In* His Sight

ISBN 978-1-4245-5216-0

Design by Chris Garborg | garborgdesign.com

Compiled and edited by Michelle Winger | literallyprecise.com

Printed in China.

16 17 18 19 20 21 22   7 6 5 4 3 2 1

LET THE
BEAUTY OF
THE LORD
OUR GOD BE
UPON US,
AND ESTABLISH
THE WORK OF
OUR HANDS
FOR US.

PSALM 90:17 NKJV

Deeper Roots

Calla lilies are beautiful flowers with wide, spotted leaves, thick stems, and bold colors. Year after year, you can watch the stunning leaves appear, and anticipate the gorgeous flowers… and then be disappointed when nothing more happens. Perhaps the soil is the problem? Calla lilies can be very particular.

It's a great picture of Jesus' parable of the sower and the seeds. Some seeds fall on rocky soil, and while God's Word is received, it doesn't take firm root and quickly withers at the sign of hardship. The seeds that are established in good soil, where the roots can go deep, not only survive, they also bear fruit.

Do you hope to see more depth in your relationship with Jesus? Do you want others to see God's beauty displayed through your life? Be encouraged to hear the words of Jesus and then allow those words to penetrate your heart deeply until you understand them. Plant yourself in fertile soil, and watch the beauty that emerges.

"THE ONE ON WHOM SEED WAS SOWN ON THE GOOD
SOIL, THIS IS THE MAN WHO HEARS THE WORD
AND UNDERSTANDS IT; WHO INDEED BEARS FRUIT
AND BRINGS FORTH, SOME A HUNDREDFOLD, SOME
SIXTY, AND SOME THIRTY."

MATTHEW 13:23 NASB

LET MY TEACHING FALL ON YOU LIKE RAIN;
LET MY SPEECH SETTLE LIKE DEW.
LET MY WORDS FALL LIKE RAIN ON TENDER GRASS,
LIKE GENTLE SHOWERS ON YOUNG PLANTS.

DEUTERONOMY 32:2 NLT

SINCE LOVE GROWS WITHIN YOU,
SO BEAUTY GROWS. FOR LOVE IS
THE BEAUTY OF THE SOUL.

AUGUSTINE

THE LORD WILL ALWAYS LEAD YOU. HE WILL
SATISFY YOUR NEEDS IN DRY LANDS AND GIVE
STRENGTH TO YOUR BONES. YOU WILL BE LIKE A
GARDEN THAT HAS MUCH WATER, LIKE A SPRING
THAT NEVER RUNS DRY.

ISAIAH 58:11 NCV

WHEN I CHOOSE TO LOOK AT EACH MOMENT
AS A MOMENT IN WHICH TO BE THANKFUL,
I WILL FIND IN EACH MOMENT BEAUTY, JOY,
AND SATISFACTION.

FLOWERS OF YOUR FAITHFULNESS ARE BLOOMING
ON THE EARTH. RIGHTEOUSNESS SHINES DOWN
FROM THE SKY.

PSALM 85:11 TPT

THE SWEETEST THING IN ALL MY LIFE HAS
BEEN THE LONGING TO FIND THE PLACE
WHERE ALL THE BEAUTY CAME FROM.

C.S. LEWIS

THEY WILL COME AND SHOUT FOR JOY ON THE
HEIGHTS OF ZION; THEY WILL REJOICE IN THE
BOUNTY OF THE LORD—THE GRAIN, THE NEW WINE
AND THE OLIVE OIL, THE YOUNG OF THE FLOCKS
AND HERDS. THEY WILL BE LIKE A WELL-WATERED
GARDEN, AND THEY WILL SORROW NO MORE.

JEREMIAH 31:12 NIV

GOD'S GRACE CAN PRODUCE IN YOU
A BEAUTY THAT WILL NEVER FADE.

MY MOUTH IS FILLED WITH YOUR PRAISE,
DECLARING YOUR SPLENDOR ALL DAY LONG.

PSALM 71:8 NIV

ALL THINGS AS THEY MOVE TOWARD GOD
ARE BEAUTIFUL, AND THEY ARE UGLY AS
THEY MOVE AWAY FROM HIM.

A.W. TOZER

FROM HIS ABUNDANCE WE HAVE ALL RECEIVED
ONE GRACIOUS BLESSING AFTER ANOTHER.

JOHN 1:16 NLT

HOW GOODNESS HEIGHTENS BEAUTY!

HANNAH MORE

Awakening the Sun

Spring is a gorgeous time of year in the northern region of the world. Snow is melting, buds are opening, and the earth appears to be coming back to life after a deep slumber.

Just as we appreciate the beauty of the season, God has a fine eye for loveliness too. He is the ultimate painter, creating a beautiful canvas all over the world as it awakes. He wants each of us to be embraced in the warmth of the sun as we are reminded of his love and care.

Look up! Turn your face toward the sun. Let its warmth rest on you. God is working in all things. Just as the sunlight touches every corner of the earth, the Lord moves in every area of your life. Allow him to do his work in you today. Take time to notice the ways in which he is touching you with his warm embrace.

WHAT A HEAVENLY HOME GOD HAS SET FOR THE SUN,
SHINING IN THE SUPERDOME OF THE SKY!
SEE HOW HE LEAVES HIS CELESTIAL CHAMBER EACH MORNING,
RADIANT AS A BRIDEGROOM READY FOR HIS WEDDING,
LIKE A DAY-BREAKING CHAMPION EAGER TO RUN HIS COURSE.
HE RISES ON ONE HORIZON, COMPLETING HIS CIRCUIT ON THE OTHER,
WARMING LIVES AND LANDS WITH HIS HEAT.

PSALM 19:4-6 TPT

I CAN DO EVERYTHING THROUGH CHRIST,
WHO GIVES ME STRENGTH.

PHILIPPIANS 4:13 NLT

GOD IS ENRAPTURED BY THE INNER BEAUTY
OF YOUR TRUE SELF.

LOVE DOES NOT DELIGHT IN EVIL BUT REJOICES
WITH THE TRUTH.

I CORINTHIANS 13:6 NIV

THE CHRISTIAN DOES NOT THINK GOD WILL
LOVE US BECAUSE WE ARE GOOD,
BUT THAT GOD WILL MAKE US GOOD
BECAUSE HE LOVES US.

C.S. LEWIS

EVERY FIELD IS WATERED WITH THE ABUNDANCE
OF RAIN-SHOWERS SOAKING THE EARTH AND
SOFTENING ITS CLODS, CAUSING SEEDS TO
SPROUT THROUGHOUT THE LAND.

PSALM 65:10 TPT

FAITH FILLS A MAN WITH LOVE FOR THE
BEAUTY OF ITS TRUTH, WITH FAITH IN
THE TRUTH OF ITS BEAUTY.

FRANCIS DE SALES

CONSIDER THE LILIES, HOW THEY GROW: THEY
NEITHER TOIL NOR SPIN; BUT I TELL YOU,
NOT EVEN SOLOMON IN ALL HIS GLORY CLOTHED
HIMSELF LIKE ONE OF THESE.

LUKE 12:27 NASB

BEAUTY SHINES FROM WITHIN. IT DRESSES
ITSELF IN HUMILITY AND WISDOM.

YOU CROWN THE EARTH WITH ITS YEARLY HARVEST,
THE FRUITS OF YOUR GOODNESS.

PSALM 65:11 TPT

IN ALL RANKS OF LIFE THE HUMAN HEART
YEARNS FOR THE BEAUTIFUL; AND THE
BEAUTIFUL THINGS THAT GOD MAKES ARE
HIS GIFT TO ALL ALIKE.

HARRIET BEECHER STOWE

THE GRASS WITHERS, THE FLOWER FADES,
BUT THE WORD OF OUR GOD WILL STAND FOREVER.

ISAIAH 40:8 ESV

WITH AGE COMES INWARD
RENEWAL AND BEAUTY.

LUXURIANT GREEN PASTURES BOAST OF
YOUR BOUNTY AS YOU MAKE EVERY HILLSIDE
BLOSSOM WITH JOY.

PSALM 65:12 TPT

BEAUTY IS NOT DEMOCRATIC; SHE REVEALS
HERSELF MORE TO THE FEW THAN TO THE MANY.
C.S. LEWIS

I LIVE BY FAITH IN THE SON OF GOD WHO
LOVED ME AND GAVE HIMSELF TO SAVE ME.

GALATIANS 2:20 NCV

YOU WERE CREATED TO BE A MASTERPIECE! YOU
ARE LOVELY AND YOU ARE LOVED SIMPLY BECAUSE
THAT IS HOW GOD MADE YOU.

KEEP TRUSTING IN YOUR RICHES AND DOWN YOU'LL
GO! BUT THE LOVERS OF GOD RISE UP LIKE
FLOWERS IN THE SPRING.

PROVERBS 11:28 TPT

BEAUTY IS A HEART MOTIVATED
BY A LOVE OF GOD.

Most Beautiful of All

If there is one thing that a woman can appreciate, it's something pretty. Shiny things easily catch our attention, and we seek to surround ourselves with beauty. There is much beauty to be found in the natural world.

There is nothing wrong with finding loveliness in our world, but if there is one thing that is more beautiful than anything else, it is the Lord God himself. His love, his mercy, his grace, and his understanding—it is nothing short of breathtaking.

Don't miss the beauty of the Lord today. Seek it. It's there to be found! You've been created to enjoy all that is exquisite, beautiful, and captivating. Give in to that desire, and find it in him! Once you have discovered the allure of it, you will find that nothing is more fetching than the Lord in his love.

HERE'S THE ONE THING I CRAVE FROM GOD,
THE ONE THING I SEEK ABOVE ALL ELSE:
I WANT THE PRIVILEGE OF LIVING WITH HIM
EVERY MOMENT IN HIS HOUSE,
FINDING THE SWEET LOVELINESS OF HIS FACE,
FILLED WITH AWE,
DELIGHTING IN HIS GLORY AND GRACE.
I WANT TO LIVE MY LIFE SO CLOSE TO HIM
THAT HE TAKES PLEASURE IN MY EVERY PRAYER.

PSALM 27:4 TPT

BLESSED ARE THOSE WHOSE STRENGTH IS IN YOU,
WHOSE HEARTS ARE SET ON PILGRIMAGE. AS THEY
PASS THROUGH THE VALLEY OF BAKA, THEY MAKE
IT A PLACE OF SPRINGS; THE AUTUMN RAINS ALSO
COVER IT WITH POOLS.

PSALM 84:5-6 NIV

NOTHING IN HUMAN LIFE, LEAST OF ALL IN
RELIGION, IS EVER RIGHT UNTIL IT IS BEAUTIFUL.

HARRY EMERSON FOSDICK

THEY SPREAD BEFORE ME LIKE PALM GROVES,
LIKE GARDENS BY THE RIVERSIDE. THEY ARE
LIKE TALL TREES PLANTED BY THE LORD,
LIKE CEDARS BESIDE THE WATERS.

NUMBERS 24:6 NLT

PEONIES IN JUNE, THE WINK OF A
QUARTER MOON, LOVING AND BEING LOVED,
THESE ARE BEAUTIFUL GIFTS FROM GOD.

THE FOUR CORNERS OF THE EARTH WERE FORMED BY
YOUR HANDS, AND EVERY CHANGING SEASON OWES
ITS BEAUTY TO YOU.

PSALM 74:17 TPT

LOVE IS LIKE A BEAUTIFUL FLOWER WHICH I MAY
NOT TOUCH, BUT WHOSE FRAGRANCE MAKES THE
GARDEN A PLACE OF DELIGHT JUST THE SAME.

HELEN KELLER

CHARM IS DECEPTIVE, AND BEAUTY DOES NOT
LAST; BUT A WOMAN WHO FEARS THE LORD
WILL BE GREATLY PRAISED.

PROVERBS 31:30 NLT

WHY CHASE AFTER THE BEAUTY THAT IS
ELUSIVE WHEN YOU CAN DWELL IN THE
BEAUTY THAT REMAINS FOREVER?

THERE IS A TIME FOR EVERYTHING, AND
EVERYTHING ON EARTH HAS ITS SPECIAL SEASON.

ECCLESIASTES 3:1 NCV

IT IS NOT THE EYE THAT SEES THE BEAUTY OF
THE HEAVEN, NOR THE EAR THAT HEARS THE
SWEETNESS OF MUSIC OR THE GLAD TIDINGS OF A
PROSPEROUS OCCURRENCE, BUT THE SOUL, THAT
PERCEIVES ALL THE RELISHES OF SENSUAL AND
INTELLECTUAL PERFECTIONS; AND THE MORE NOBLE
AND EXCELLENT THE SOUL IS, THE GREATER AND
MORE SAVORY ARE ITS PERCEPTIONS.

JEREMY TAYLOR

THE LORD SEES NOT AS MAN SEES: MAN LOOKS
ON THE OUTWARD APPEARANCE, BUT THE LORD
LOOKS ON THE HEART.

I SAMUEL 16:7 ESV

BEAUTY BECOMES EVIDENT IN THOSE WHOSE
RECOGNIZE THAT THE HEART IS PRONE TO UGLINESS.

THE LORD IS NEAR TO ALL WHO CALL ON HIM,
TO ALL WHO CALL ON HIM IN TRUTH.

PSALM 145:18 NIV

BEAUTY SEEN IS NEVER LOST,
GOD'S COLORS ALL ARE FAST.

JOHN GREENLEAF WHITTIER

WE ARE NOT SAYING THAT WE CAN DO THIS WORK
OURSELVES. IT IS GOD WHO MAKES US ABLE
TO DO ALL THAT WE DO.

2 CORINTHIANS 3:5 NCV

A TRULY BEAUTIFUL PERSON IS ONE
WHO SEES BEAUTY IN OTHERS.

Come Away

Some say that romance is dead. It's not for God: the lover of our souls. He desires nothing more than time with his creation! It can be a little uncomfortable to have his gaze so intently upon us though. We're nothing special, after all! Not beauty queens, academic scholars, or athletic prodigies of any kind. We might not be musical, or crafty, or organized. Our house might be a mess, and we could probably use a manicure.

Do you feel a bit squeamish under such an adoring gaze? There is good news for you! You are, in fact, his beautiful one! And he does, indeed, want to bring you out of the cold winter. He's finished the watering season and it is finally—*finally*—time to rejoice in the season of renewal.

Why do you feel uncomfortable under the gaze of the one who loves you more than anyone else ever could? The time has come. He is calling you, regardless of how unworthy you may think you are. Will you arise and come away with your beloved? He is waiting for you!

MY BELOVED SPEAKS AND SAYS TO ME:
"ARISE, MY LOVE, MY BEAUTIFUL ONE,
AND COME AWAY, FOR BEHOLD, THE WINTER IS PAST;
THE RAIN IS OVER AND GONE.
THE FLOWERS APPEAR ON THE EARTH,
THE TIME OF SINGING HAS COME."

SONG OF SOLOMON 2:10-12 ESV

O LORD OUR GOD, LET YOUR SWEET BEAUTY
REST UPON US AND GIVE US FAVOR.

PSALM 90:17 TPT

THE FLOWER OF YOUTH NEVER APPEARS
MORE BEAUTIFUL THAN WHEN IT BENDS
TOWARD THE SUN OF RIGHTEOUSNESS.

MATTHEW HENRY

BE STILL AND KNOW THAT I AM GOD.
I WILL BE EXALTED AMONG THE NATIONS,
I WILL BE EXALTED IN THE EARTH!

PSALM 46:10 NIV

REAL BEAUTY IS NOT WHAT THE EYES CAN
BEHOLD BUT WHAT THE HEART CAN HOLD.

THIS IS THE CONFIDENCE THAT WE HAVE TOWARD
HIM, THAT IF WE ASK ANYTHING ACCORDING TO
HIS WILL HE HEARS US. AND IF WE KNOW THAT HE
HEARS US IN WHATEVER WE ASK, WE KNOW THAT WE
HAVE THE REQUESTS THAT WE HAVE ASKED OF HIM.

1 JOHN 5:14-15 ESV

THOSE WHO DIVE IN THE SEA OF
AFFLICTION BRING UP RARE PEARLS.

CHARLES SPURGEON

YOU WILL BE ADORNED WITH BEAUTY AND GRACE,
AND WISDOM'S GLORY WILL WRAP ITSELF AROUND
YOU, MAKING YOU VICTORIOUS IN THE RACE.

PROVERBS 4:9 TPT

TRUE BEAUTY HOLDS TIGHT THE HAND
OF ITS COMPANION—GRACE.

THE LORD DIRECTS THE STEPS OF THE GODLY.
HE DELIGHTS IN EVERY DETAIL OF THEIR LIVES.

PSALM 37:23 NLT

THE BEST AND MOST BEAUTIFUL THINGS IN THE
WORLD CANNOT BE SEEN OR EVEN TOUCHED –
THEY MUST BE FELT WITH THE HEART.

HELEN KELLER

EVERYTHING I AM WILL PRAISE AND BLESS THE
LORD! O LORD, MY GOD, YOUR GREATNESS TAKES
MY BREATH AWAY, OVERWHELMING ME BY YOUR
MAJESTY, BEAUTY, AND SPLENDOR!

PSALM 104:1 TPT

GOD MAKES BEAUTIFUL THINGS
OUT OF THE DUST.

NO EYE HAS SEEN, NO EAR HAS HEARD, AND NO
MIND HAS IMAGINED WHAT GOD HAS PREPARED
FOR THOSE WHO LOVE HIM.

I CORINTHIANS 2:9 NLT

KIND WORDS CAN BE SHORT AND EASY TO SPEAK,
BUT THEIR ECHOES ARE TRULY ENDLESS.

MOTHER TERESA

CLAP YOUR HANDS, ALL YOU NATIONS;
SHOUT TO GOD WITH CRIES OF JOY.
FOR THE LORD MOST HIGH IS AWESOME,
THE GREAT KING OVER ALL THE EARTH.

PSALM 47:1-2 NIV

TO BE THE RECIPIENT OF A LOVE THAT IS
EVERLASTING MEANS THAT YOU CAN NEVER FALL
OUT OF FAVOR WITH THE ONE WHO LOVES YOU.

Hidden Beauty

Beauty is a powerful influencer in the lives of women. We are constantly bombarded with images and messages of what beauty is and what it should be. Even if we are confident in who we are, it can still be difficult not to give in to the subtle thoughts of not being good enough.

The awful truth about outward beauty is that no matter how much time, attention, and investment you put into it, beauty can never really last. Our appearance inevitably changes over time, and our physical beauty does fade.

In a world where we are constantly told to beautify ourselves so we will be noticed, the concept of adorning the hidden person of the heart sounds almost make-believe. But what it comes down to is the truth that the most important opinion we should seek is the opinion of our Creator. It might sound trite or cliché, but when we step away from the distraction of the media circus and all the lies it's told us, the truth becomes clear.

You were made to delight the heart of God. Nothing delights him more than your heart, turned toward your Savior and clothed in the imperishable beauty of a peaceful spirit flowing with gentleness, kindness, and goodness.

LET YOUR ADORNING BE THE HIDDEN PERSON OF
THE HEART WITH THE IMPERISHABLE BEAUTY OF
A GENTLE AND QUIET SPIRIT, WHICH IN GOD'S
SIGHT IS VERY PRECIOUS.

I PETER 3:4 ESV

THANK YOU FOR MAKING ME SO WONDERFULLY
COMPLEX! YOUR WORKMANSHIP IS MARVELOUS—
HOW WELL I KNOW IT.

PSALM 139:14 NLT

GOD VALUES A BEAUTY THAT THE WORLD
KNOWS LITTLE ABOUT.

THE LORD BLESS YOU, AND KEEP YOU;
THE LORD MAKE HIS FACE SHINE ON YOU,
AND BE GRACIOUS TO YOU;
THE LORD LIFT UP HIS COUNTENANCE ON YOU,
AND GIVE YOU PEACE.

NUMBERS 6:24-26 NASB

CHARACTER IS ALWAYS LOST WHEN A HIGH
IDEAL IS SACRIFICED ON THE ALTAR OF
CONFORMITY AND POPULARITY.

CHARLES SPURGEON

PEOPLE ARE LIKE GRASS; THEIR BEAUTY
IS LIKE A FLOWER IN THE FIELD.

1 PETER 1:24 NLT

WHERE ELSE COULD OUR EYES FIND SUCH
BEAUTY AND PURITY AS THEY DO UPON THE
FACE OF JESUS?

MY FLESH AND MY HEART MAY FAIL,
BUT GOD IS THE STRENGTH OF MY HEART
AND MY PORTION FOREVER.

PSALM 73:26 NASB

THERE ARE TIMES WE NEED ONLY TO CRAWL INTO
OUR ABBA'S LAP AND ALLOW HIS LOVE AND
PROMISES TO ENVELOP US IN COMFORT.

BEHOLD, YOU ARE BEAUTIFUL, MY LOVE, BEHOLD, YOU ARE BEAUTIFUL!

SONG OF SOLOMON 4:1 ESV

YOU HAVE MADE US FOR YOURSELF, O LORD,
AND OUR HEARTS ARE RESTLESS UNTIL
THEY REST IN YOU.

AUGUSTINE

IN MY TROUBLE I CRIED TO THE Lord,
AND HE ANSWERED ME.

PSALM 120:1 NASB

TRIALS TEACH US WHAT WE ARE; THEY DIG UP THE
SOIL, AND LET US SEE WHAT WE ARE MADE OF.

CHARLES SPURGEON

TO ALL WHO MOURN IN ISRAEL, HE WILL GIVE A
CROWN OF BEAUTY FOR ASHES, A JOYOUS BLESSING
INSTEAD OF MOURNING, FESTIVE PRAISE
INSTEAD OF DESPAIR.

ISAIAH 61:3 NLT

JOY ALLOWS US TO SEE BEAUTY
IN THE MIDST OF CHAOS.

THOUGH THEY STUMBLE, THEY WILL NEVER FALL,
FOR THE Lord HOLDS THEM BY THE HAND.

PSALM 37:24 NLT

LEAVE BEAUTY EVERYWHERE YOU GO.

Beautiful Layers

The art of a painting lies not in what you see, but in the process that has gone into making it what it has become. Usually a painting begins with inspiration: an idea or emotion that wants to be expressed. It proceeds with sketching, color, texture, and variations in between. A painter rarely produces exactly what they originally pictured.

Our life with God can be like a painting. It begins with our faith. Our belief in Jesus sets up our canvas, but the Scriptures call us to add to the depth of our faith by applying colors of goodness, knowledge, and self-control. The beauty emerges as we add perseverance, godliness, affection, and love. These things take time to develop. They can involve mistakes, and they can end up making us look very different than how we started.

Jesus has begun a good work in you. Have faith in his saving grace. Make the effort to become more beautiful by applying goodness, perseverance, and love to your life.

MAKE EVERY EFFORT TO ADD TO YOUR FAITH
GOODNESS; AND TO GOODNESS, KNOWLEDGE; AND
TO KNOWLEDGE, SELF-CONTROL; AND TO SELF-
CONTROL, PERSEVERANCE; AND TO PERSEVERANCE,
GODLINESS; AND TO GODLINESS, MUTUAL
AFFECTION; AND TO MUTUAL AFFECTION, LOVE.

2 PETER 1:5-6 NIV

THE KING WILL GREATLY DESIRE YOUR BEAUTY;
BECAUSE HE IS YOUR LORD, WORSHIP HIM.

PSALM 45:11 NKJV

YOUR LORD IS A FIRE: DO NOT LET YOUR HEART
BE COLD, BUT BURN WITH FAITH AND LOVE.

JOHN OF KRONSTADT

YOUR EYES WILL SEE THE KING IN HIS BEAUTY
AND VIEW A LAND THAT STRETCHES AFAR.

ISAIAH 33:17 NIV

THE WIDEST THING IN THE UNIVERSE
IS NOT SPACE; IT IS THE POTENTIAL
CAPACITY OF THE HUMAN HEART.

A.W. TOZER

HONOR AND MAJESTY SURROUND HIM;
STRENGTH AND JOY FILL HIS DWELLING.

I CHRONICLES 16:27 NLT

THE IDEALS WHICH HAVE ALWAYS SHONE BEFORE
ME AND FILLED ME WITH THE JOY OF LIVING
ARE GOODNESS, BEAUTY, AND TRUTH.

ALBERT EINSTEIN

LIGHT IS SWEET; HOW PLEASANT
TO SEE A NEW DAY DAWNING.

ECCLESIASTES 11:7 NLT

YOU CREATE YOUR BEAUTY THROUGH YOUR
BEHAVIORS, YOUR ACTIONS, AND YOUR ATTITUDE.

SET ME AS A SEAL UPON YOUR HEART,
AS A SEAL UPON YOUR ARM.

SONG OF SOLOMON 8:6 NRSV

GOD LOVES US JUST BECAUSE WE ARE HIS.
AND WE LOVE HIM BECAUSE HE LOVED US.
IT'S JUST THAT SIMPLE.

ONE THING I ASK FROM THE LORD,
THIS ONLY DO I SEEK:
THAT I MAY DWELL IN THE HOUSE OF THE LORD
ALL THE DAYS OF MY LIFE,
TO GAZE ON THE BEAUTY OF THE LORD
AND TO SEEK HIM IN HIS TEMPLE.

PSALM 27:4 NIV

BEAUTY IS THE GIFT OF GOD.
ARISTOTLE

FOR THE Lord GOD IS OUR SUN AND OUR SHIELD.
HE GIVES US GRACE AND GLORY.
THE Lord WILL WITHHOLD NO GOOD THING
FROM THOSE WHO DO WHAT IS RIGHT.

PSALM 84:11 NLT

IT'S NOT HOW MUCH WE HAVE, BUT HOW
MUCH WE ENJOY, THAT MAKES HAPPINESS.

CHARLES SPURGEON

SING ABOUT A FRUITFUL VINEYARD:
I, THE LORD, WATCH OVER IT;
I WATER IT CONTINUALLY. I GUARD IT DAY
AND NIGHT SO THAT NO ONE MAY HARM IT.

ISAIAH 27:2 NIV

YOU MIGHT BE IMPERFECT,
BUT YOU ARE PERFECTLY YOU.

All Things Beautiful

We've probably all heard an older gentleman declare that his wife is more beautiful now than the day they married. And we likely thought, *He needs glasses.* What we fail to recognize in our outward-focused, airbrushed society, is that time really does make things beautiful. More accurately, time gives us better perspective on the true definition of beauty. Spending time with those we love affords us a glimpse into the depth of beauty that lies within. So while the external beauty may be fading, there is a wealth of beauty inside.

God's Word says that he makes all things beautiful in his time. *All* things. Whatever situation you are facing right now, it has the potential to create beauty in you. Perseverance, humility, grace, obedience—these are beautiful. But there's more. The beauty God creates in us cannot be fully described in human terms! There is eternal beauty to be found.

When you are met with challenges, run to your Father and sit in his presence. When you dwell there, you reflect his character. Allow the difficulties in your life to become a catalyst for true beauty.

HE HAS MADE EVERYTHING BEAUTIFUL IN ITS TIME.
HE HAS ALSO SET ETERNITY IN THE HUMAN HEART;
YET NO ONE CAN FATHOM WHAT GOD HAS DONE
FROM BEGINNING TO END.

ECCLESIASTES 3:11 NIV

BLESSED BE THE Lord, BECAUSE HE HAS HEARD
THE VOICE OF MY SUPPLICATION.
THE Lord IS MY STRENGTH AND MY SHIELD;
MY HEART TRUSTS IN HIM, AND I AM HELPED.

PSALM 28:6-7 NASB

IF INSTEAD OF A GEM, OR EVEN A FLOWER, WE
SHOULD CAST THE GIFT OF A LOVING THOUGHT
INTO THE HEART OF A FRIEND, THAT WOULD BE
GIVING AS THE ANGELS GIVE.

GEORGE MACDONALD

IN YOUR NAME THEY REJOICE ALL DAY,
AND BY YOUR RIGHTEOUSNESS THEY ARE EXALTED.
FOR YOU ARE THE GLORY OF THEIR STRENGTH.

PSALM 89:16-17 NASB

BEAUTY WITHOUT VIRTUE
IS LIKE A ROSE WITHOUT SCENT.

THE LORD ALWAYS KEEPS HIS PROMISES;
HE IS GRACIOUS IN ALL HE DOES.

PSALM 145:13 NLT

LET GOD'S PROMISES SHINE
ON YOUR PROBLEMS.

CORRIE TEN BOOM

SHE OPENS HER MOUTH IN WISDOM, AND THE
TEACHING OF KINDNESS IS ON HER TONGUE.

PROVERBS 31:26 ESV

BEAUTY BEGINS IN THE HEART WHEN YOU RECOGNIZE
THAT YOU ARE NOTHING WITHOUT CHRIST.

SEE HOW VERY MUCH OUR FATHER LOVES US,
FOR HE CALLS US HIS CHILDREN,
AND THAT IS WHAT WE ARE!

I JOHN 3:1 NLT

THERE ISN'T ROOM FOR FEAR ALONGSIDE
PERFECT LOVE. IF WE ABIDE IN THE LOVE
OF JESUS, THEN WE HAVE PERFECT LOVE
IN US, AND FEAR MUST SURRENDER.

YOU ARE A CHOSEN PEOPLE, A ROYAL PRIESTHOOD,
A HOLY NATION, GOD'S SPECIAL POSSESSION,
THAT YOU MAY DECLARE THE PRAISES OF HIM
WHO CALLED YOU OUT OF DARKNESS INTO HIS
WONDERFUL LIGHT.

I PETER 2:9 NIV

SPREAD LOVE EVERYWHERE YOU GO. LET NO ONE
EVER COME TO YOU WITHOUT LEAVING HAPPIER.
MOTHER TERESA

WE CAN CONFIDENTLY SAY, "THE LORD IS MY HELPER;
I WILL NOT FEAR; WHAT CAN MAN DO TO ME?"

HEBREWS 13:6 ESV

WHATEVER SITUATION YOU ARE FACING
RIGHT NOW, IT HAS THE POTENTIAL TO
CREATE BEAUTY IN YOU.

THESE THINGS I HAVE WRITTEN TO YOU WHO
BELIEVE IN THE NAME OF THE SON OF GOD, THAT
YOU MAY KNOW THAT YOU HAVE ETERNAL LIFE, AND
THAT YOU MAY CONTINUE TO BELIEVE IN THE NAME
OF THE SON OF GOD.

I JOHN 5:13 NKJV

IN THIS WORLD IT IS NOT WHAT WE TAKE UP,
BUT WHAT WE GIVE UP THAT MAKES US RICH.

HENRY BEECHER

Beauty from Hardship

Creating a diamond is, for the transforming coal, a long and painful process. Simple carbon undergoes an immense refining pressure that produces a wholly new creation. We might just see a cloudy rock at this stage, but there is another refining step to be taken. After the stone-cutter does his work, a precise shining diamond emerges: magnificent, glittering, brilliant.

When we endure hardship, the long and painful process can seem unfair. But our life stories are written by a compassionate Creator who is crafting a masterpiece. He is refining us, like the diamond, into something entirely beyond our imagination. And we can rejoice in the beauty he is creating. You may not see it now, but it's coming soon.

Let God show you the emerging beauty under the surface of the hardships you face. You will come out of the situation stronger and brighter, shining for God if you submit to his process and trust his skilled and loving hands.

LET PERSEVERANCE FINISH ITS WORK SO
THAT YOU MAY BE MATURE AND COMPLETE,
NOT LACKING ANYTHING.

JAMES 1:4 NIV

LET US THEN APPROACH GOD'S THRONE OF GRACE
WITH CONFIDENCE, SO THAT WE MAY RECEIVE
MERCY AND FIND GRACE TO HELP US IN
OUR TIME OF NEED.

HEBREWS 4:16 NIV

WE HARBOR A BEAUTY THAT SURPASSES ANY
WORLDLY DEFINITION: GRACE, PATIENCE,
COMPASSION, GENEROSITY, KINDNESS. ALL OF
THESE MAKE US BEAUTIFUL IN GOD'S EYES.

BEFORE HE MADE THE WORLD, GOD CHOSE US TO
BE HIS VERY OWN THROUGH WHAT CHRIST WOULD
DO FOR US; HE DECIDED THEN TO MAKE US HOLY
IN HIS EYES, WITHOUT A SINGLE FAULT—WE WHO
STAND BEFORE HIM COVERED WITH HIS LOVE.

EPHESIANS 1:4 TLB

DOUBT DISCOVERS DIFFICULTIES WHICH
IT NEVER SOLVES; BELIEVE IS THE WORD
WHICH SPEAKS LIFE.

CHARLES SPURGEON

HUMBLE YOURSELVES IN THE SIGHT OF THE LORD,
AND HE WILL LIFT YOU UP.

JAMES 4:10 NKJV

WE NEED NEVER SHOUT ACROSS THE SPACES TO AN
ABSENT GOD. HE IS NEARER THAN OUR OWN SOUL,
CLOSER THAN OUR MOST SECRET THOUGHTS.

A.W. TOZER

THE EARTH CAUSES PLANTS TO GROW, AND A
GARDEN CAUSES THE SEEDS PLANTED IN IT TO
GROW. IN THE SAME WAY THE LORD GOD WILL MAKE
GOODNESS AND PRAISE COME FROM ALL NATIONS.

ISAIAH 61:11 NCV

THE TRUE BEAUTY OF A PAINTING LIES
NOT ONLY IN WHAT YOU SEE, BUT IN THE
PROCESS THAT HAS GONE INTO MAKING IT
WHAT IT HAS BECOME.

IN MY TROUBLE I CRIED TO THE Lord,
AND HE ANSWERED ME.

PSALM 120:1 NASB

THE ART OF BEING HAPPY LIES IN THE POWER OF
EXTRACTING HAPPINESS FROM COMMON THINGS.

HENRY BEECHER

"THE FATHER GIVES ME THE PEOPLE WHO ARE
MINE. EVERY ONE OF THEM WILL COME TO ME,
AND I WILL ALWAYS ACCEPT THEM."

JOHN 6:37 NCV

LOVELY FLOWERS ARE THE SMILES
OF GOD'S GOODNESS.

WILLIAM WILBERFORCE

I AM CONFIDENT OF THIS VERY THING, THAT HE
WHO BEGAN A GOOD WORK IN YOU WILL PERFECT IT
UNTIL THE DAY OF CHRIST JESUS.

PHILIPPIANS 1:6 NASB

GOD DELIGHTS IN YOU. HE SINGS OVER
YOU: NOTES AND REFRAINS HERE AND
THERE AS YOU GO ABOUT YOUR DAY.

BREATHTAKING BRILLIANCE AND AWE-INSPIRING
MAJESTY RADIATE FROM HIS SHINING PRESENCE.
HIS STUNNING BEAUTY OVERWHELMS ALL WHO COME
BEFORE HIM!

PSALM 96:6 TPT